The Dot Man:
George Andrews of Madison, Georgia

J. Richard Gruber

MORRIS
MUSEUM of ART

1 9 9 4

PEACE IN THE VALLY FOR ALL
Oil on canvas board, 16 x 20 in.

This volume has been published in conjunction with the exhibition "The Dot Man: George Andrews of Madison, Georgia," organized by the Morris Museum of Art, curated by J. Richard Gruber.

Editor:	Louise Keith Claussen
Design:	Lydia Inglett
	Vincent Bertucci
	Morris Communications Corporation
Photography:	Eric Olig
	Morris Communications Corporation
ISBN:	0-9638753-3-7

CONTENTS

THE DOT MAN: GEORGE ANDREWS OF MADISON, GEORGIA

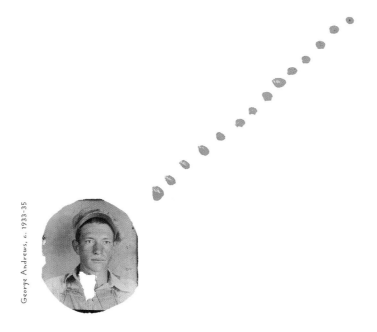

George Andrews, c. 1933–35

"He's like a brush filled with dripping paint walking around looking for some place to place a drop..."

Benny Andrews [1]

FOREWORD

Within its permanent collection devoted to painting in the South, the Morris Museum of Art focuses on a broad range of Southern art and artists. Because the art of the South is as endlessly diverse as the South itself, the collection encompasses both trained and untrained artists, the formally educated and the self-taught.

In presenting "The Dot Man: George Andrews of Madison, Georgia," we offer an opportunity to explore an intriguing body of work made by the patriarch of a highly creative family of artists and writers, a family richly blessed with talent and deeply rooted in the soil of rural Georgia.

George Andrews, former sharecropper, father of ten, lifelong artist, is reaching an artistic milestone in his eighty-fourth year — his first solo retrospective exhibition in a museum. With the generous cooperation of Benny Andrews, son of George Andrews and noted academically-trained artist, a comprehensive selection of George's works, from paintings on canvas to dot-covered plates and shoes, has been assembled.

In organizing this exhibition, J. Richard Gruber, Deputy Director of the Morris Museum, devoted many hours to recording oral histories and videotaping interviews and sites in Morgan County, Georgia, where a two-room cabin near the town of Madison was home to a family that recognized and nurtured the creative spirit. In his essay, he explores the ways in which the art of George Andrews is closely tied to the land where he was born, a small Southern community where social boundaries were defined and defied, and the ways his art is also linked to his family, for whom poverty was no deterrent to creative expression.

As Dr. Gruber points out, art was simply part of the routine of life for George Andrews and his family. It was not an elevated, elitist art; no gallery walls gave it boundaries or limitations. Instead, art was an element of family life, documenting the collective dreams and experiences of two generations, and demonstrating their God-given creative abilities.

The Morris Museum of Art is pleased to present this exhibition, and to celebrate the achievements of a singularly expressive self-taught Georgia artist. ●

Louise Keith Claussen
Director, Morris Museum of Art

George Andrews, c. 1935-36

"Daddy read a lot—the newspaper, detective and western magazines, and novels and comic books. He was Plainview's 'closet' reader, since reading wasn't 'manly.' As a child, Daddy had learned to play the violin, or 'fiddle,'and guitar. He also learned to draw and 'paint' pictures."

Raymond Andrews [2]

INTRODUCTION AND ACKNOWLEDGEMENTS:

This exhibition, and the opportunity to work with George Andrews, evolved from a series of conversations with Benny Andrews which took place during the late 1980s. At the time, while I was serving as director of the Memphis Brooks Museum of Art, Benny was working with curator Patricia Bladon to plan the exhibition "Folk: The Art of Benny and George Andrews." That exhibition was presented in Memphis in the fall of 1990 and traveled to museums, galleries and cultural centers in six other cities over the next two years. The art of George Andrews, until then known primarily in Madison and Atlanta, Georgia, was introduced to diverse new museum and gallery audiences throughout the country.

Last year, during a visit with Benny in his Athens, Georgia, studio, we talked about his father, then eighty-two years old, and the significant body of work he had produced since the opening of the "Folk" show. I was shown a series of Andrews family portraits and a wide range of new paintings and objects which had been created during the past three years. Except when slowed by problems with his eyesight, George still actively painted on a regular basis. Reviewing the extensive range of work completed since 1990, and seeking to present a retrospective consideration of his life and career in Morgan County, we began to plan an exhibition for the Morris Museum of Art. This is that exhibition.

Now approaching his 84th birthday, George Andrews maintains his daily routines. In addition to reading his papers, talking with friends in town and visiting the Madison Post Office, he paints and creates new works including the refinement of "Sitting Bull," an elaborate installation which fills the center of his living room. He often spends part of the day responding to visitors and representatives from the media and art world. Except when he is trying to paint, he seems to enjoy these interactions and exchanges.

We appreciate the interest shown by George Andrews and his willingness to work with members of the museum staff on diverse elements of the exhibition and the related video. His son, Benny, has actively supported all phases of the planning, research and presentation of this exhibition and has contributed enormously to the success of this project. We thank both George and Benny as well as other members of the Andrews family.

In Augusta, this show has been actively supported and advanced by Louise Keith Claussen, Director of the Morris Museum, who also served as editor of this publication. Estill Pennington, Curator of Southern Painting, recognized the importance of this artist's work and supported the exhibition concept from an early date. Catherine Wahl, Registrar, coordinated the complex and often challenging details associated with the movement and cataloguing of the show. Jim Tar and Gail Kuehn have installed a challenging exhibition with imagination and energy. Ann Rowson's educational programs have been planned to extend the exhibition and related issues to school and adult audiences in Augusta and the region.

Vince Bertucci and Lydia Inglett, of Morris Communications Corporation, have developed a catalogue design which is distinctive and most appropriate for the art and the whimsical humor of the Dot Man. Eric Olig's photography adds signficantly to the catalogue and the exhibition. Reginald Wells, Director of Morris Corporate Communications, Bo Roberts and Jeff Barnes have been equally committed to the production of the George Andrews video which accompanies the exhibition.

For all of us, at the museum, and those elsewhere seeking to advance the recognition and understanding of the art of the South, the support and encouragement of William S. Morris III is, as always, deeply appreciated.

Finally, the determination and vision of George Andrews has been an inspiration to us. This catalogue is dedicated to him and to the remarkable spirit of the Andrews family of Morgan County, Georgia. ●

J. Richard Gruber

The path of George Andrews' life and career can be traced along the county road which winds from Plainview to Madison, Georgia. Born in Plainview in 1911, George Andrews has never lived far from the place of his birth. He travels rarely, refuses to spend a night away from Morgan County, and has never been outside the state of Georgia. He is firmly rooted in the soil of Morgan County.

This is the same soil which nurtured his parents, his siblings and, during the 1930s and 1940s, his own children. It is the soil he learned to work as a child and later cultivated as a sharecropper and family farmer. It is an essential element of the environment which inspires his art.

Place, and the strong ties of family to place, are integral to the culture of the South. "One place comprehended," Eudora Welty observes, "can make us understand other places better."[3] The rural setting of Plainview and the surrounding areas of Morgan County might not appear, on the surface, to be an inspiring location for artists and writers. However, Morgan County has inspired and influenced four generations of Andrews family members.

Plainview does not appear on most highway maps. However, the presence of the Andrews family established its significance on the creative landscape. A two-room cabin, built on family land in 1935, served as the home for much of this activity. In his book, *The Last Radio Baby*, Raymond Andrews described the placement of the family cabin on the farm and its relationship to the highway: "The road located a hundred yards or so from the front of our house ran to the main road, called the 'crossroads,' which was about a quarter of a mile from our house and led to town."[4]

This simple dirt road ran past the family farm, intersected at the "crossroads," the highway leading into Madison, and continued to the Plainview Baptist Church and the Plainview School, the public institutions of the community. For years, the life of the Andrews family centered on this small stretch of Georgia road and the farms surrounding it. The town of Madison, four miles to the north, provided a lively urban center for the family during the 1930s and 1940s. Atlanta, with its thriving black community and educational opportunities, loomed at the far end of the highway.

Plainview, like many small Southern communities, was forever altered as mechanization reshaped the nature of farming, and the northern migration pulled the rural workforce toward major industrial centers. George Andrews was forced eventually to leave his home in the country and he moved to the north side of Madison, about five miles from Plainview. He has lived in the same neighborhood, not far from the town square of Madison, for more than thirty five years.

An artist at heart since his childhood, George Andrews moved from Plainview but never abandoned the spirit of his family's community. His farming labors ended, his children grown and moved on, he turned increasingly toward the production of art after his move into town. The works included in this exhibition were created after the move to Madison, most since 1970. Little remains from the earlier years. At that time his work was not regarded as "art."

The highway from Madison to Plainview has served as an axis for George Andrews. He has seldom moved far from that axis. In Madison, the "Dot Man" lives and paints in a familiar and supportive environment. His many friends and acquaintances are nearby and often stop by to visit. And Plainview remains, just down the highway. ●

GEORGE ANDREWS, ARTIST

Until 1990, the art of George Andrews was known primarily in the Madison area and, to a lesser degree, in Atlanta's arts and African-American communities. Through the continuing efforts of his son, artist Benny Andrews, his work has received broader recognition in recent years. "Folk: The Art of Benny and George Andrews," an exhibition curated by Patricia Bladon and organized by the Memphis Brooks Museum of Art, traveled nationally to museums and cultural centers from 1990 to 1992. The self-taught artist and former share-cropper was finally recognized by the American museum world as he approached his eightieth birthday.

In the spring of 1994, as this essay is written, an Atlanta gallery is presenting George Andrews' first urban gallery exhibition and sale.[5] "The Dot Man: George Andrews of Madison, Georgia," organized by the Morris Museum of Art in association with George and Benny Andrews, is the first retrospective exhibition of his work. Both exhibitions are being presented in Georgia. George Andrews still refuses to leave the state of his birth and will not sleep away from his home in Morgan County.

Awareness of George Andrews' art is growing at a time when museums, encouraged by a new generation of curators and scholars, are recognizing anew the complexity and importance of the visions of self-taught and "out-sider" artists. This recognition, evident in a diverse range of recent museum exhibitions and publications, is per-haps most significantly documented in an exhibition organized by the New Orleans Museum of Art, "Passionate Visions of the American South: Self-Taught Artists from 1940 to the Present." The exhibition, being pre-sented in a national tour during 1994 and 1995, is the result of years of field research in the South by curator Alice Rae Yelen. Over 270 works by eighty artists were included in the New Orleans venue of "Passionate Visions."

Writing in the exhibition's catalogue, Yelen suggests a context for these works: "Southern self-taught artists born before World War II were primari-ly raised in rural environments, deeply rooted and often irrevocably connected to their land, communities, traditions, and families." In general, these artists work "without knowledge of the artistic mainstream," do not seek the accep-tance of the art world and, importantly, "do not consider themselves artists nor do they typically intend to sell their work." Self-taught artists work, Yelen concludes, "in response to inner visions" and "to visual stimuli from all aspects of their daily lives."[6]

Although it may be possible to suggest common elements in the lives of Southern self-taught artists, the work of the best of these artists is difficult to classify. There is a resulting quality to self-taught art which reaches beyond traditional museum audiences. Lucy Lippard, in her study of multicultural-ism in the American art world, found that self-taught artists may actually be best equipped to "provide intricate maps of reality, of daily and spiritual life" because they live in the "real" world, not the art world. More main-stream artists may, in contrast, remain confined to the "intimidatingly clean or luxurious art gallery or grandly insti-tutionalized museum—outside the flow of life." Lippard suggests that self-taught and vernacular art "gives people a way to speak for themselves across the moat that protects the high-art world from knowing what 'the people' really think and see."[7]

As with other contemporary artists, the work of the self-taught artist must be considered within the specific context of the artist's life, goals and vision. This is particularly evident with an artist like George Andrews, whose background and experiences are rich and quite com-plex. The details of his life and his experiences in rural Georgia are cer-tainly unique. ●

George Cleveland Andrews was born, one of seven children, in Plainview on August 1, 1911. Four of his siblings, Christine, Mamie, Quiller, and Gary, died during childbirth, as often happened during this era in the South.

James Orr House

Plainview Baptist Church

Old Plainview School house

George's older brother, Fred, was born in 1909. His younger sister, Beatrice, was born in 1917. His parents were James Orr and Jessie Rose Lee.

James Orr, known locally as Mister Jim, was born on December 17, 1879 to William Jackson Orr and Sara Angeline Few Orr. Of Scotch-Irish descent, his father and older brother, William, ran a large cotton plantation, known as Oaks Plantation and the "Orr Place," several miles outside of Madison. The plantation was dominated by a large, white classical revival mansion. Plainview grew up around this plantation and the "big house" dominated the community for years. George Andrews matured in the shadow of the plantation house, his father's home, and raised his own family in a nearby cabin. Jim Orr graduated from high school in Madison and attended several Southern colleges. He was fond of riding his bicycle during his youth, once leading a group of friends on a cycling trip through Texas and into Mexico.

James Orr met Jessie Andrews, who was several years his senior, on the plantation just after the turn of the century. At the time, she was married to Eddie Andrews, one of the hired farm hands. Although she remained married to Eddie Andrews until his death in 1917, Jessie and James Orr quickly became a couple and remained so, unmarried, for more than fifty years. Jessie Rose Lee was born in Maxey, Georgia, on March 7, 1872, to Minerva Jones, who was black, and a father who was half white and half Indian. As a tribute to her heritage, her father added "Wildcat Tennessee" to her name. When she was eleven years old, her family moved from Maxey to

Barrows Grove, not far from Plainview.

By all accounts, the mother of George Andrews was a remarkable woman. Noted for her striking beauty, high cheekbones, fair skin and long black hair, she seemed to command attention. Her grandson, Raymond Andrews, wrote a book about her life and referred to her often in his publications: "Jessie was a free spirit and grew up precocious in both body and mind, but she was remembered most for her long-haired beauty… Legend had her to be the most beautiful woman ever to roam the region or strut the streets of Madison."[8]

In Jessie's honor, James Orr donated two acres of land for the construction of a new Plainview Baptist Church, which was completed in 1916. She became known as "Mother" of this church or just "Mother Jessie." This church and the adjoining graveyard, where Jessie is buried today, became the spiritual center of Plainview and an integral part of the life of the Andrews family. By this time, they were also raising three children. Although they lived in adjoining houses, there was little question about their relationship and their defiance of the standards of Morgan County.

Changes were occurring in the Orr family fortunes by this time. Jim Orr's father died in 1910. Soon after, other problems, including the arrival of the boll weevil in the region, contributed to a decline in agricultural production. Growing debts on the family properties forced the sale of the plantation house and much of the adjoining land in 1918. Jim moved out of the big house and into modest quarters on the remaining farmland near Jessie's home.

George Andrews and members of the family still recall stories about the selling of a plantation "which had once stretched within the county from Plainview to the community of Buckhead, land so vast it was discussed in terms of miles rather than acres."[9]

George attended elementary school in a simple wooden structure, which is still standing, near the grounds of the Baptist Church in Plainview. Here, in the first grade, he remembers creating his first acknowledged works of art: "I was just around seven years old. First, Mama bought me some crayons, and I would draw pictures and things in school. And my teacher would look at it, she say, 'It's really good.'" When his teacher asked George to draw a vase with flowers he responded: "If I see it I could draw it." She encouraged him by saying "Use your imagination. You got a good imagination."[10]

Like any proud child, George returned home and reported his teacher's comments to his mother, adding that he would need more crayons. He clearly remembers his mother's response: "I'm sending you down there to learn a lesson! I ain't sending you down there to draw for the teacher!" When George replied, in defense, that his teacher suggested that "one of these days it would be valuable if I learnt how to art" she offered a direct, and rather threatening, conclusion to the discussion. "And Mama said, 'Well, you stop that drawing, and you go to reading and writing, that's what you do.' She said, 'If you don't, I'm gonna put you out here in the field."[11]

Although she did not offer much support for his natural abilities as an artist, George Andrews loved his mother dearly and recalls her with great fondness. Curiously, his mother also seems to have been the person most responsible for his leaving school and turning to a life of farm labor. His parents disagreed sharply about the importance of education. James Orr, the college educated son of a plantation owner, wanted to pay to send his children to the Booker T. Washington High School, Atlanta's first black public high school.

Jessie refused to allow her children to leave Plainview and argued that, as black children, they did not need a higher education. It was not uncommon, during that period in the segregated South, for black children to receive only an elementary school education. As a result, both George and Fred dropped out of elementary school after learning to read and write. George completed the third grade and was working in the fields by the time he was ten years old. From that time his life would be dominated by manual farm labor and by a continuing struggle to survive. His sister, Beatrice, attended Burney Street High School in Madison but did not graduate.

Had his father prevailed and sent his children to Atlanta for schooling, George Andrews might have experienced a radically different life. The opportunities available in Atlanta, then a growing center for the education of blacks, might have encouraged him to pursue training as an artist or to seek other opportunities during a changing time in the South. Many of his own children, encouraged by their mother, did enjoy these opportunities in Atlanta, and beyond.

George, who inherited his father's love of reading the daily newspapers, especially the *Atlanta Constitution*, continued his own education by reading. He learned to work the fields and read as time allowed. He became self-educated and remained aware of events taking place beyond the boundaries of Morgan County. He also pursued his continuing interest in drawing and art: "I still had drawing on my mind. We didn't call it art, we called it drawing."[12]

After laboring in the fields he often returned home and, with the approval of his mother, drew with available materials. He used his mother's "bluing," a cleaning powder compound, and fabricated brushes from simple components. "I cut me a little stick about that long and then got me a little rag and wrapped it around there with a string. That's what I dipped in that bluing. And I made some pretty pictures out of it. And so Mama got interested then."[13]

Later, as a young man, he used the same basic materials to paint large images of biplanes on local barns. Benny Andrews recalls that "long before any of us had any ideas of becoming

James Orr (Detail)

Andrews family cabin

professional artists, my father would go out late at night when we were all asleep and paint double winged planes on the sides of deserted barns."[14] In the morning, these memorable images, viewed with amusement, were publicly regarded as "mysterious" apparitions.

In private, it seems that the residents of Plainview recognized the creative hand and imaginative vision of George Andrews. His response to the vacant barns of Morgan County reflected his art interests as well as his active sense of humor. In the context of Southern studies, these efforts stand in sharp contrast to the activities described in William Faulkner's noted fictional account of Ab Snopes' avenging assaults on the barns of his home county in "Barn Burning," written in 1938.

Using only available materials, often scraps of paper and discarded wooden fragments, George continued to experiment with his creative gifts, producing small drawings and objects which were casually given away or simply discarded when completed. Art was, it seems, a process, a way to create and demonstrate skill and talent. The finished product was considered disposable. Though regarded as a rather curious talent, his skills were recognized by those who knew him. However, there was no question that George's artistic interests were subordinated to the pressing needs of daily survival. Work came first. Art always followed.

When he was sixteen years old, George met Viola Perryman, his future wife. Also raised on a working farm which she had loved, she looked forward to the day she would be able to raise her own children in a similar environment. She had grown up in a house full of books, magazines and newspapers. She dreamed of becoming a writer. At the age of sixteen she married George Andrews, who was a charming young man of seventeen who also loved farms and farming. Their energies were soon devoted to raising a family and to working the soils of Georgia, first as family farmers and then as tenant farmers. George's painting and Viola's writing would have to wait.

Years later, after encouraging her children's creativity, Viola Andrews finally was able to become a writer. She also found time to reflect upon her marriage and her young family: "The only thing that we had was youth and hope. Whenever we could spare a few dimes over our meager food and clothes, we bought one or two pencils, a 5 cent package of paper and a 10 cent box of colored crayons. The children, from the time they could hold a pencil, drawed and colored. They showed it to me. I praised it every time. I was no artist… I only knew they had done their best and were worthy of praise."[15]

George and Viola Andrews eventually became the parents of ten children. In 1935, a two-room wooden home was built for them on land near the house of Jessie Andrews and not far from James Orr's cabin. When they moved into the house there were four children, Harvey, Benny, Sister and Raymond. By the next year there was a fifth, a daughter, Shirley. This would remain the Andrews family home until 1943, when they moved to a nearby farm to begin working as sharecroppers.

This small cabin, expanded when the aging Jim Orr moved his house to the rear of their structure, served as the center of the Andrews family life during a critical period of time. Cousins, neighbors, friends and countless local characters filled the house and yard with activity. Still standing along the deserted dirt road, the house, and the spirit that filled the house, appear as regular elements in the art and writings created by the Andrews family. The rugged materials, heavy textures and muted colors of this structure became a part of the Andrews family legacy.

Raymond Andrews later described a warm environment in these simple rooms during his favorite time there: "A day wouldn't go by when Benny and I didn't pull out our cardboard boxes from under the bed and 'go to work' on them… Daily Benny and I reread and 'straightened out' my boxes of collectibles. Yet what I enjoyed best was sitting in the room alone, straightening out my boxes while listening on the radio to a football or baseball game. Often on a Sunday afternoon during lay-by time or late fall, rather than go into town I would stay home just for this reason. It was my favorite time of all—listening to the radio while straightening out all my boxes."[16]

Although members of the Andrews family may not have known it at the time, cabins and tenant farm houses of this type attracted the interest of a growing number of artists and photographers during the 1930s. At issue was the plight of the Southern farmer during the Depression, especially the difficulties of the tenant farmer and the subsistence farmer. Photographers, including Dorothea Lange, Margaret Bourke-White and Russell Lee, roamed the backroads of America recording these structures.

In the summer of 1936, not long after the Andrews family moved into this house, two young white men, Walker Evans and James Agee, visited Hale County, Alabama, to document the condition of sharecroppers working in that region. Originally commissioned by *Fortune* magazine as an article, their collaborative effort was eventually published as *Let Us Now Praise Famous Men*. Agee often struggled with his intensive emotional response to these houses and to the often desperate lives encountered within: "If I could do it, I'd do no writing at all here. It would be photographs; the rest would be fragments of cloth, bits of cotton, lumps of earth, records of speech, bits of wood and iron, phials of odors… I'll do what little I can in writing. Only it will be very little. I'm not capable of it; and if I were, you would

not go near it at all. For if you did, you would hardly bear to live."[17]

In reality, the houses and hardship living conditions encountered by Agee, Evans and others were little different from those experienced by the Andrews family during these same years. However, there was a critical difference. George and Viola Andrews labored, under equally oppressive conditions, often enhanced by racial tensions, to raise a proud and unified family. They refused to demonstrate a public sense of desperation. Despite their poverty, they displayed a significant level of pride and nurtured hope for the future. Benny Andrews later poignantly explained to his brother Raymond, "You and I were too naive to know we couldn't make it."[18]

More than naivety, the Andrews children were filled with a unique sense of confidence. "We were always one step away from starvation year after year," Benny recently wrote, "and though I'm sure we'd have made it through no matter what, our strong supportive family helped us to do more than just make it through. Not perfect by any means, it was a family who believed in a future through education and hope." His parents were the basic source of this belief: "Our mother, Viola was the rock, the steadying influence that gave us both direction and faith in ourselves as worthy individuals. Our father, George, gave us the creative and dreamy side." Although they were often viewed as "weird" by their neighbors, local social attitudes "didn't deter us from reading, drawing and dreaming."[19]

Though they were poor, their house

James Orr's two room addition onto the family cabin.

was filled, to an exceptional degree, with magazines, newspapers and books. George was a voracious reader and Viola had been raised in a household filled with reading materials. *The Atlanta Constitution* was a daily staple. *Life*, *Look*, *Collier's* and *The Saturday Evening Post* were passed around, studied and saved. On Saturday, George would buy copies of black newspapers, including the *Chicago Defender* and the *Pittsburgh Courier*, as well as magazines such as *Ebony*, from a black vendor in Madison.[20]

Plainview's tenant farm houses were often papered inside with newspapers and magazines. Walls were covered with words and images, and cracks and chinks were stuffed with papers. Raymond Andrews remembered that when visiting other homes with his mother he used to search for reading materials. "Many houses were wallpapered with newspaper (sometimes even the funnies!), which would have me standing on chairs to read. Into every house I was taken I went looking for something to read, but with few exceptions the reading material in all of the houses was on the wall… or in the cracks."[21]

In the Andrews house, however, drawings and family writings commonly covered the walls. A type of living collage evolved. George's later collages, incorporating newspaper images, and Benny's signature collaged paintings, layered with fabric and clothing, may have evolved quite naturally from these walls as well as from the family penchant for always using the materials at hand. The creative expressions of the family literally filled the space. Viola constantly encouraged the children to write, to draw and to share their work with the family.

George remembers returning from work in the fields, exhausted, hoping to rest for the next day of labor. His children, however, wanted him to draw pictures and to tell them stories. And, despite his exhaustion, he felt that he couldn't refuse. "We loved to hear Daddy's stories," Raymond recalled, "because even a familiar one had a different ending. The great anticipation was, How will it end this time?"[22] George often continued into the night, drawing, telling the stories they loved and sharing his visions with the children. These resulting images were then tacked or nailed directly onto the walls, nurturing the children's confidence to add their own drawings and stories to the family gallery.

Art, for George Andrews and his family, became a part of the routine of life. It was not an elevated, elitist art. Because there were no museums nearby, the boundaries of art remained relatively undefined, and unlimited. Art was instead an element of family life, documenting the collective dreams and experiences of two generations, as well as a demonstration of God-given creative abilities. After completion, a new work might be nailed to the wall, recycled into another new work or saved by Viola.

Both Benny and George regularly created drawings in the dirt, commonly using nails as drawing tools. Benny remembers learning to do this from George, marveling at his father's ability to quickly pull images from the soil of Georgia with a nail or stick. George, in turn, remembers that Benny, scheduled to labor in the fields with the rest of the family, could often be found hiding under cotton plants, drawing on the ground with his nail, an activity he favored over the picking of cotton.

While the Andrews family grew, and as the Depression continued to exert a toll on the farming communities of central Georgia, George and Viola Andrews dreamed about owning and working a farm of their own. However, because of the poor economy and their own lack of funds for equipment and farm animals, they had to become sharecroppers on a neighboring farm. The family moved to another house in 1943 and entered a period of even more intensive labor. The older children experienced the life of the black sharecropper and planned a future away from the rural life of Georgia. And, as Benny recalls, they continued to dream: "To us, imagining that we were more than

we were—poor, black sharecroppers—was like a game. We could afford to dream of being whatever we wanted to be. We had nothing to lose."[23]

After the war years, a number of factors, including the maturing of the older children and the appeal of urban life in Atlanta's black neighborhoods, contributed to the dispersal of the Andrews family. One after another, Plainview lost its hold on the children. The oldest son, Harvey, moved to Atlanta in the summer of 1945, returning often to tell about the wonders of the city. Raymond, who left home for Atlanta in 1949, at the age of 15, was amazed by Harvey's description of "colored picture shows" and "colored drugstores" in Atlanta where "the colored could order milkshakes and sit down at the tables inside and eat, rather than taking what they bought and eat it outside" as was the rule in Madison.[24]

After graduating from Madison's Burney Street High School in 1948, Benny left to attend Fort Valley State College for two years, enlisted for service in the Air Force and then completed art school at the Art Institute of Chicago. Watching the older children leave, Viola reviewed the options for her remaining children, including their limited chances for an education in Morgan County. She also considered the continuing problems in her relationship with George. In 1953, Viola and George Andrews separated and she moved to Atlanta with the remaining children.[25] George was left behind, in Morgan County. He never considered leaving. ●

With the move of his family to Atlanta, George Andrews entered a period of rapid and dramatic change in his life. His years as a farmer, and his direct connection to the soils of Morgan County, ended in the early 1950s. He obtained a job working for the city of Madison, initially commuting into town from a house he shared with his family. When Viola and the children moved to Atlanta, he moved into Madison to live closer to his work and his friends.

In his new job for the city George painted street signs. Working out of a poorly ventilated basement location, he eventually contracted chemical poisoning from the lead-based paint. The illness was severe and lengthy. He was transported on a regular basis to the medical center in Augusta for treatment and returned to Madison. After this occurrence, because he was no longer able to work on a regular basis, he depended on Social Security benefits for his income. When he returned to Madison to recuperate he was offered, and accepted, living spaces in the city's government housing project. He has lived and painted in this same area, on the same street, for more than thirty five years.

Over the following years, with the reduction of family pressures, an enhanced awareness of his own mortality and, for the first time in his adult life, a great deal of available time for his art, he experimented with his painting. Experienced at using the materials at hand, he began to paint rocks, as he had in the past, for himself. Friends and acquaintances saw these rocks and began to acquire them

from him. Brightly colored, dot-filled rocks began to appear around Madison. Often placed outside, the rocks with their bright colors and signature dot patterns began to be recognized in the city. The retiring artist, whose works in the past had been completed for himself and his family, slowly gained recognition in Madison.

People in the Madison area began to call George Andrews the "Dot Man." He was gradually becoming more of a public figure, acknowledged for his art. In the past, he had painted images of biplanes with temporary materials on barns, scratched drawings in the dirt, drawn on available materials and constructed objects from scraps. With the painting of rocks in Madison, and the positive reaction to these colorful images, he enjoyed a previously unexperienced form of public acceptance. Encouraged by this recognition, he continued to experiment with colors and new patterns.

Prior to his move to Madison in the 1950s, his art had been impermanent and known only to a small group of

people in Plainview. Little, if anything, exists from the earlier period. After the move to town, and after his recognition as the "Dot Man," a new concern for the permanence of the object became evident in his art. As his residence in the city became a gathering place for friends and visitors, more people saw his work in progress and witnessed the newest pieces as he completed them.

As a next logical step, he expanded the range of his work to include porch furniture and other items on his porch and around the yard. Soon his furniture was decorated with colors and dot patterns. Gradually, as he experimented with these pieces, and as friends visited and talked about the painted furniture, he began to incorporate written lines and witty phrases on the furniture. This appears to be the first use of writing as an element of design in his painting. The phrase "Sit your bottom on my bottom," included on a chair in this exhibition, adds humor and a sense of narrative to a simple piece of metal furniture. A lawn chair like this, a standard item on front porches and yards throughout the South, was easily recognized and invited usage. It also must have prompted a great deal of conversation.

The extremely social nature of his life and his living environment directed much of what the artist began to paint. The shy George Andrews developed an enhanced public profile after his move to Madison. His many friends, both men and women, began to drop by with greater frequency. His lady visitors soon discovered that their shoes and purses might be sacrificed to

George's artistic cause, leading people to remark that if an item didn't move George would paint it. The shoes, boots and purses included in this exhibition show a whimsical flair and a continuing bold sense of color and decorative exploration. Empty liquor bottles, a byproduct of the gaiety of the social gatherings at "Gee's" house, also were painted and incorporated into his living environment.

The "Dot Man" continued to be eclectic in his interests and his creative explorations. Other objects began to follow—found objects, scraps of styrofoam packing materials, plates, platters, gelatin molds and other household items—as the raw materials of his art. The styrofoam trays used by groceries and restaurants, often discontinued now because of environmental concerns, served as a convenient material for the artist. These flat trays presented an ideal surface for the Dot Man's brush. Examples in this show include images of pigs, dancing snakes, human figures and a religious motif, "At The Cross I Bow."

Friends who visited his home began to bring objects along for George's use. "People bring me," he noted," all kinds of things. Mostly I like them unpainted little animals and dolls you get in the ten cent store."[26] These were either incorporated into his tableau or were painted and returned to the individual. Spinning objects, including fans and whirligigs, and a wall clock with a moving pendulum offered the opportunity to explore color, pattern and motion. Animal forms, including chickens, pigs, lizards and turtles, in a variety of materials, were painted and enlivened with his sense of spirit, creating an eclectic barnyard for the old farmer from Plainview.

Patricia Bladon, the curator of the first museum exhibition of George Andrews' work, offered a concise summation of the value of these works: "The paintings and decorative objects which typically fill George Andrews' home are so authentic in formal values that his aesthetic consciousness is unquestioned." Noting that he is "totally aware of…

symmetry, balance and repetition" she pointed to his use of compartmentalization which she found "akin to the patchwork designs of many storytelling quilts."[27] His sense of color, pattern and composition continued to develop.

Public recognition and acceptance, even on a limited scale, brought a growing confidence to his painted forms. His role in the community began to change, as he explained more than ten years ago: "Since people been seeing the rocks I paint in houses of folks all over town, more and more people ask me about my work. I go down to the postoffice to pick up my mail and they don't call me 'G'

anymore. They call me Mr. Andrews." And, as he suggested, he became increasingly recognized as an artist: "Folks sure are funny about you when they think you're an artist. I tell them, 'I'm no artist, I just do these things,' but I guess I am an artist. I'm painting too."[28]

"Calendar Page Dog," one of the earliest works included in this exhibition, was produced by painting over an inexpensive framed image of a hunting dog (PAGE 28). A series of painted lozenges rings the picture frame and a pattern of dots and waving lines encroaches, across the surface of the glass, upon the image of the dog. Here, still working primarily in a decorative manner, he has simply enhanced a mass-produced art object. In "Last Supper," he moved more aggressively into the picture plane of a mass produced icon (PAGE 29), layering his colors onto the surface and emphasizing the elements of perspective which are missing from his own work. Like the majority of the works in this exhibition, these paintings are undated.

The transition from decorative painting to the creation of complete compositions was encouraged during the 1980s, beginning about 1985 or 1986, by his son Benny, who brought George small canvas boards for experimentation and use in his art. Benny, recognizing that his father was "like a brush filled with dripping paint," offered George a place to deposit the paint as well as the images which sprang from his imagination. It also seems that once he was regarded as an artist, George Andrews wished to live up to the title, painting at a furious pace to create works befitting his new status.

The variety, complexity and visual sophistication of the images he has produced during the last ten years, beginning when he was 73 years old, seem driven by a unique fusion of energy and inspiration. "I just sit here in my chair," he explained "and look at the things I'm doing and get ideas. Sometimes late at night an idea hit me and I jump up and do it."[29] The immediate world around him, including elements of life in Madison and rural Morgan County, inspires much of this work. In "2 Cain Snakes Dong The Buggy" (PAGE 30) a pair of snakes stand, vertically, doing a dance with forked tongues projecting and imaginary hands joined. A colorful painted field serves as a border, framing the composition, with the title inscribed below.

A favorite subject for the artist, and a reflection of his many years in the country, is the pig. His pigs, perhaps inspired by dreams and visions, certainly reflecting his keen sense of humor, perform acts not normally associated with the pigs of Morgan County including flying, sky diving and hanging from trees. In "The Kissing Pigs O Boy Har" two pairs of colorful pigs are aligned, in a symmetrical pattern, surrounded by dots, squiggles and a border of red, blue and black brush strokes. "The Pig Tree" (PAGE 31) offers a recurring Andrews motif, pigs hanging from or growing on trees. In "2 Hogs Skis Jumping O Boy," airborne pigs float to earth, protected by harnesses and parachutes, which protrude into the painted border.

Other paintings deal with more abstract patterns and compositions, demonstrating his growing mastery of the two-dimensional surface and his expansive use of color. "Scramble Art" is based upon a composition of interlocking triangular forms, surrounded by regular lines of dots, leading the eye to a border of primary color patterns (PAGE 32). Works like "I Got All My Eyes On You" (PAGE 33) and "Pleas Done Try to Button Me Down" also use triangular compositional patterns, placed within a painted border, to create overlapping planes which suggest a three dimensional surface. The numerous eyes in the former work also suggest a type of curse or jinx, perhaps a version of casting the "evil eye."

These triangular motifs and abstract elements were also applied to a unique, handmade wooden chair (PAGE 34) designed by his grandson, Christopher Andrews. Christopher, a boat builder and architect who operates a firm in New York City, is the son of Benny Andrews and a member of the third creative generation of the Andrews family. Painting the chair with a blue ground (his favorite color), George Andrews decorated each plane of the chair with patterns of yellow, red and white. Unaware of color field painting, cubism and other forms of abstraction, George Andrews creates works which suggest elements of the most advanced art movements of the twentieth century.

Although he has grown used to life in the city of Madison he is concerned, like countless other people of his age, about urban violence and crime. His daily newspapers and his magazines recount horrible crimes in great detail and describe seemingly endless tales of drug abuse. As a result he, like a number of other self-taught artists, creates works as social commentaries. "On Dope Talk" addresses these concerns. Three young men, of diverse ethnic backgrounds, reject the use of beer, marijuana, crack cocaine, cigarettes and needles, shown aligned along the top of the canvas. By rejecting these diverse addictions, they will contribute to the return of a productive, work-oriented society.

Armed violence is the subject of "The Poor Little Gun," which depicts an unemployed gun, unable to "hold a job" because it had been fired six times. Sitting daily at his window or on his front porch, Andrews witnesses the decline of his own neighborhood, the government housing project he has regarded as home for more than three decades. He has begun to worry about the safety of his own environment even in historic Madison, Georgia.

An interest in specific African-American themes reflects his own heritage and an awareness of current issues of racial empowerment and multiculturalism in American society. Since his youth in the segregated South numerous civil rights programs, many initiated in Atlanta, where his younger children matured, have contributed to a changing environment in the South and in the nation. "Black Is Beautiful," depicting upright, proud young black figures, is a conscious tribute to the popular black pride movement. More subtle is the collaged image, "Africa Queen," which features a powerful black female adorned with jewelry and surrounded by dots and a distinctive border (PAGE 35). The use of a photographic image for the figure marks an interesting departure for the

artist and reflects his constant exposure to media images.

The more complex realities of his family's mixed racial heritage also informed his art. George suffered racial prejudice and slurs from members of both the black and white races because of his light skin and mixed parentage. His own children endured similar difficulties. In his idyllic painting (PAGE **36**), "The White Rabbit Married the Color Rabbit," is he metaphorically portraying a marriage between his mixed-blood mother, Jessie Rose Lee Wildcat Tennessee, and his Scotch-Irish father, James Orr, the son of a Georgia plantation owner? Despite the length of their relationship, his parents never married. Additionally, his wife, Viola, was the daughter of a black man who had been ostracized by his own family for marrying a light-skinned black woman. In the world of the artist, however, all could work out for the best, as he notes on his painting, "And Lives a Happy Life. That Right."

Dreams provide the inspiration for many of his most significant paintings. His early years in Plainview were directly linked to the strong heritage and traditions of the African-American slaves of the Georgia plantations. Within the culture of his own family, great emphasis was placed upon the value of dreams. Viola Andrews, a deeply Christian woman and active member of her church, takes dreams and visions quite seriously. George has learned to remain open to his dreams and to use the dreaming process to direct and inform his paintings. Often he will read and

think about specific subjects, planning what he hopes will be a dream devoted to that topic. When he experiences such a dream he will awaken and quickly sketch the image, then return to complete it later in the day.

John Beardsley, writing in the catalogue which accompanied "Black Folk Art In America, 1930-1980," a groundbreaking exhibition organized by the Corcoran Museum, points to the importance of spiritual voyages and visions in the work of self-taught artists. "The voyage represents both a desire for deliverance—from the physical limitations of life—and an affirmation of belief that the world is full of majesty and mystery and worthy of scrutiny… The vision, too, promises redemption and deliverance and is similarly without self-pity." Even for those without strong religious beliefs, the vision commonly shows the future and is "based on the hope of the salvation and even apotheosis of the maker in another, more perfect world." [30]

"Peace in the Valley for All," one of George Andrews' dream paintings, certainly illustrates Beardsley's points. Two powerful bluebirds are shown soaring over the mountaintops while other bluebirds appear to be nesting, settling in to the life of the valley. Bright, cheerful colors prevail, while the sun and golden clouds float in the distance (PAGE **2**). In contrast, "The Valley or Dry Bones" is filled with denuded trees covered with skulls, while skeletons and skulls litter the ground below, around the base of the trees (PAGE **37**). A harsh yellow background, a color often used to portray psychological disturbance or psychic pain, fills the

central picture plane while the light of a remote sun seems obscured by the presence of soaring vultures or evil birds. The artist leaves little doubt about his preferred destination.

Visions of a different type are also common in the work of George Andrews. "The Walking Bridge from Space" was, he recently confirmed, literally painted from a dream. A festive series of girders, painted, of course, with his dots, moves across an unidentifiable terrain on long legs. The legs are shown stretching out with wiggling toes seemingly leading the way forward (PAGE **38**). Is this the invention of a race of space beings or perhaps a bridge for the transition into space, or into the afterlife? It is a humorous, colorful work which nevertheless combines many of his traditional elements in a confident and powerful visual composition.

Although not a religious person, George Andrews has painted a number of iconographic religious images. His mother was a stalwart founder of the Plainview Baptist Church and his wife, Viola, has been an active member of that church and her current church in Atlanta, where she has taught Sunday School for thirty nine years. He has been, in other words, no stranger to the messages and imagery of the church. "Jesus on the Croos" presents a fairly conventional interpretation of the crucifixion, with Christ on a central crucifix, surrounded by dots, and two suggested crosses in the distance, also composed of dots. Evil, the other side of this religious concern, has been depicted as well in works such as "The Devil and His 2 Sons." ●

In 1989, at the age of 78, George Andrews initiated an ambitious, long term project devoted to painting the history of the Andrews family in an extended series of portraits. The series began with a self-portrait which he completed for inclusion in "Folk: The Art of Benny and George Andrews," the touring museum exhibition of his art. His son Benny, who suggested that George consider painting the family, supplied stretched canvases for his father's use. Benny watched as his father expanded the concept from their initial conversation, including the painting of the Andrews family tree to accompany the series. Working from 1989 to 1991, he painted a significant number of portraits, but the series remains uncompleted. The paintings are being shown, together, for the first time in this exhibition.

"This is George Andrews O Boy Ha Ha," began the series in a vibrant and almost baroque manner, with the self-portrait of George surrounded by colorful dots, lines, circular forms and geometric elements which seem to explode around him (TITLE PAGE).

The canvas, one of his largest, seems too small to contain all that happens here. The outline of George's figure was first sketched on the canvas by Benny, making this a collaborative effort. George then painted what amounts to a dual self-portrait.

The Dot Man, wearing his ever-present cap, faces the viewer directly, arms at his side, surrounded by the forms and colors of his vivid imagination. Energy and color seem to float, spin and perhaps even whistle in the air around

This is the Andrews Family - Andrews Family Tree (Detail)

him, suggesting an aura of creativity and dynamism. The body, he seems to say, may be that of an elderly, pale skinned, stooped African-American sharecropping father of ten, but inside is a dynamo, a steaming, pulsing source of energy and visions that can hardly be contained by the body we see.

In the spirit of many advanced modern painters, George Andrews gives the viewer a self-portrait of psychological,

perhaps even psychic, depth that transcends simple portraiture.

A portrait of his son, "This Is Benny Andrews," followed (PAGE 40). His son the artist is shown, brush in hand, looking off into the distance, perhaps contemplating his next painting or one of his future projects. The light skin of Benny's face, surrounded by his white hair and beard, emerges from the dark and somewhat mysterious field of activity which surrounds him. George, the self-taught artist, sometimes chides his famous son for attending art schools to learn to paint and draw. In comparison, George explained, he is a "natural" artist who needed no training to paint.

This portrait suggests that the confident father, now able to exhibit in museums next to his son, has decided to surround Benny with a world drawn from his own imagination and talent. In the upper right corner, above the eyes and mouth of a floating spirit or face, George inscribes "This is Benny Andrews paintings by his farth George." To the left, next to Benny's head, he writes "Play but done start nought old boy my son Benny watching you Har."

Benny hovers over a distinctive landscape below, filled with golden trees, animals, flowers and architectural forms. In a carefully bordered panel, George offers a text to accompany this vision. "You are look at the land or the golden 4 trees of a geart valley or sunshine by George Andrews." Clearly, the painting of the portrait of Benny has elicited another vision, which George has documented and included as part of the total composition. It is a fascinating and complex work which demonstrates the range

George Andrews, 1933

Benny Andrews

Nene Humphrey

of George's vision and his ability to match the creativity of his famous son.

Soon after completing the portrait of Benny, George painted Benny's wife, the artist Nene Humphrey. There are strong similarities in color and composition between the two which suggest that George envisioned these portraits to be shown as a pair, in the manner of historical family portraits, perhaps hanging in the couple's New York or Athens homes. "Nene Humphrey" (PAGE 41) presents his daughter-in-law sitting in a chair, reading, wearing a red dress with a brightly colored pattern which contrasts with the dark background filled with his signature dots and marks. Nene, who is nationally recognized as an abstract sculptor, is not shown in the studio or at work. She is depicted as a reader, like so many other members of the Andrews family, and as a thinker. George, not normally an admirer of abstract art, or other artists, is quite intrigued by Nene's work.

"My Daddy Like His Paper (James Orr)," painted in 1990, depicts his father seated in a straight backed wooden chair, reading a newspaper (PAGE 39). He is shown wearing light trousers, a patterned shirt and a white hat with a striped band, apparently the clothing of a plantation owner's son. What appears to be a gold necklace or chain contrasts, interestingly, with his darkened skin. George's white father, of Scotch-Irish descent, is shown with darker skin than George, Benny or Nene possess in their portraits.

Vines wind around James Orr, flowers float over his head and a column, covered with painted dots, stands to the right, suggesting that his father is seated on the front porch of the family's plantation house (the house he was forced to sell). A regular reader of the Atlanta paper, he is shown gazing directly at the viewer with the following inscription, written in pencil and red paint, on his paper: "The Atlanta Constitution The Moring Paper My Dad like his paper he wood in joy read it but he passe but was love by all who know him His name was James Orr but was call Mr Jim He once was a big land oner well all good things do come to a inn so by we see you."

In contrast to his father's seated portrait, George painted his mother standing, wearing a blue dress and what appears to be an apron, holding a long flower. This large flower seems to merge into or explode into an array of related floral forms which cover the picture plane. "I Love You Mother Dear (Jessie Rose Lee Wildcat Tennessee)" was completed in 1991 (PAGE 42). His mother's Indian blood is suggested in her long black hair braid. She also wears jewelry and, like many of these portrait figures, is depicted wearing a wrist watch on her right arm.

George's mother was a widely recognized and influential figure in Morgan County, especially in the Plainview area. She was a founder of the Plainview Baptist Church, known as "Mother Jessie" to its members, and is prominently buried in the graveyard behind the church. As a pointed reminder of the legacies of the segregated South, she is buried in Plainview while James Orr, George's father, is buried in his family's plot in the white cemetery, near the historic district in Madison. Inscribed, in the upper right

James Orr

Jessie Rose Lee Wildcat Tennsee

Viola Andrews

corner of the painting, is "I love you mother dear Gee. Her Son." Below, he wrote "Stop look read better knon as Jessie Rose Lee Wildcat Tennsee and That Right."

The most ambitious painting in this series was completed in October of 1991. "This Is The Andrews Family," usually called "The Family Tree" by George, presents the children of George and Viola Andrews filling the branches of a sturdy tree. (PAGE 43). Though he had been painting family portraits and thinking about the family for almost two years, George had not envisioned this type of group portrait. The picture came to him, he has stated, in a dream. Rather than a complex genealogical chart or the type of family tree diagram so well known to Southern families, George literally painted a tree and filled it with his children.

In the foreground beneath the tree, George the hardworking farmer, wearing coveralls and his trademark cap, works a plow being pulled by his mule. "Get up Nellie Bell" he yells to a spot-

ted mule pulling a red plow. Behind him, closer to the tree and its root system, is Viola Andrews, shown holding a baby wrapped in a blanket inscribed with "a nought baby" across its surface. Five children are shown on the heaviest branch of the tree, which is growing out toward the right edge of the picture plane. Harold, Raymond, Benny and Harvey are seated, legs dangling, while Valeria stands, waving out to the viewer. On the upper, left branch Johnny, Delores, Veronica and Shirley are more precariously placed.

"The Family Tree" is filled with George's family and with an extensive range of his favorite subjects and visual motifs. In the lower right corner, the Andrews cabin in Plainview, shown with its welcoming front porch and smoke filtering from the chimney, is included, almost a member of the family. Below it is written "This is the Andrews family 4 girls 6 boys Douno Benny and George Andrews October 4 1991 So look all you want." Creeping vines and flowering shrubs form the side borders. Floating over George's head are his bluebirds and a pair of

hanging tree pigs. A somewhat abstract, cloudlike element at the top is meant to suggest leaves. Dots and waving lines fill all remaining vacant spaces, pulling all of these elements together into a unified composition.

"My Lovig Wife (Viola Andrews)," also painted in 1991, (PAGE 44), presents Viola in a formal seated position, facing left, clutching her purse in her lap. Dressed in Sunday clothes and wearing a fine hat, his deeply religious wife is presented in the foreground with the Plainview Baptist Church, a central element in her life, shown in the background. A wandering vine, adorned with flowers, creates a delicate border for the work, perhaps suggestive of Victorian decorative detailing. After many years of association with the Plainview Baptist Church, Viola moved to Atlanta in 1953 and joined the Hunter Hill Baptist Church.

After her move to Atlanta, Viola studied theology at the Atlanta School of Biblical Studies. Now proudly associated with Hunter Hill Baptist Church for 39 years, she is also a dedicated teacher of Bible studies. The relationship be-

Harvey Andrews

Shirley Andrews

Valeria Andrews

tween his mother and father was concisely described by Benny: "Viola Andrews, my mother, was the perfect match for my father in terms of his being the humorous and idealistic artist. She was very serious, wrote all the time and encouraged us to 'draw and paint like your father.' She was the first one of us to actually get her work published. She won a prize from a chain of grocery stores for her writing of 'What America Means To Me…'"[31]

Harvey Andrews, the oldest son, is shown in a military uniform, at attention, facing forward toward the viewer (PAGE 45). Handsome in his crisp blue uniform coat and white hat, the embodiment of loyalty and responsibility, he is presented as an ideal oldest son. An American flag, painted as a rigid field of brilliant color, balances Harvey's stiff pose in the right half of the composition. A small white truck, dwarfed by the flag, reflects and repeats the white of his hat and uni-

form pockets and suggests, perhaps, the fruits of his son's labors. Harvey was the first child to leave Plainview, moving to Atlanta in July of 1945.

"Shirley Andrews" presents another child in uniform, in this case a daughter who has accomplished much as a professional nurse (PAGE 46). Shirley's starched white uniform and bright nurse's cap stand out from the painted dots and lines of the background. She holds a clipboard, identified as "Chart" and is surrounded by George's version of the symbols of her profession. As a child, her brother Raymond explained, Shirley had attracted attention for her beauty: "'Oh, she's sooo pretty.' That's all the grown folks could ever think to say when they saw little Shirley (some going so far as to even call her 'Shirley Temple')."[32]

"Valeria Andrews" is also painted in a uniform and presented in a pose that is identical to the one used in Shirley's portrait (PAGE 47). Wearing her blue postal worker's uniform, Valeria holds a stamped letter, inscribed with her name, and gestures with her left hand.

She is shown with a pocket filled with pens and pencils and wears a wrist watch on her right arm. Her necklace is enlivened by an actual rhinestone brooch which is pinned to the canvas surface. Valeria, known in the family as one of George's favorites, is shown with a intense field of color, almost a halo, floating behind her head.

A different type of clothing and symbolism is presented in the painting "Joe." Harold Andrews, called Joe in the family, was a practicing Black Muslim and was portrayed in this context by his father (PAGE 48). Joe was named after the prominent boxer Joe Louis, a powerful and heroic figure to the children of the Andrews family. The work is inscribed "This is Joe Going but not forgotting." Joe, who was killed in an automobile accident, is buried in the Plainview Baptist Church graveyard, next to his grandmother, Jessie Rose Lee Wildcat Tennessee. The presence of his mother and his son in the Plainview

Harold Andrews

Raymond Andrews

cemetery contributes to his continuing ties to the spirit of Morgan County.

George portrayed his son "Raymond Andrews," pencil in hand, about to begin a writing project (PAGE 49). Wearing a bright blue shirt, his dark hair and goatee framing his glasses and eyebrows, Raymond beams radiantly out to the viewer. On the paper before him George has written: "Now For My Nex Book Now Let Me Thank." Arrayed behind him on a shelf are four of his books, with one, *Baby Sweets*, prominently placed next to his elbow.

This painting, one of the last family portraits, was completed in 1991. Late that year, in November of 1991, Raymond Andrews committed suicide in Athens, not far from Morgan County. A successful and influential writing career ended at the same time that a sense of tragedy and intensive grief descended upon the Andrews family. With Raymond's death the Andrews family lost a son and brother and also lost its most dedicated historian.

Explaining the motivations for his writing, Raymond referred to his family's place in the history of the modern South: "My books deal with a slice of America which I feel too little is known of, the rural and small town Southern blacks. Those who stayed behind, thus forsaking the Promised Land… America's black roots in this country are in the South, a region whose foundation was built by black sweat, muscle, soul and blood. These are the people I'm of, write of, and want my readers to know of."[33]

By the end of 1991, George Andrews found himself unable to continue painting the family portraits. Moving through the family tree chronologically, he finished the portraits of Joe and Shirley and stopped painting the series. All of the Andrews children were included in "The Family Tree." The tribute to his parents, his wife and his children consumed much of a three-year period. Then eighty years old, he found it difficult to work on such a scale. The loss of his son Raymond added to this burden and seems to have made it impossible to conclude the project. ●

Benny at the family cabin, 1977

In the late spring of 1994, as George Andrews approaches his 84th birthday, he watches the world respond to the paintings and objects he has created. In May, during the opening of his Atlanta gallery exhibition, he mingled with the urban art crowd, the type of crowd often portrayed in Benny's paintings, and listened to the polite conversation of collectors and museum dignitaries. That night, after the opening, Benny drove him back to Madison, where he slept surrounded by his latest creations. Other people, including many in his own family, may have joined the rush to Atlanta, but George Andrews stayed, and only feels comfortable when he spends the night in his home in Morgan County.

After a hard life of farming and sharecropping, working to support a large family under difficult circumstances, George Andrews seems to view his recognition as an "artist" with a mixture of pride and a certain amusement. Although his eyesight sometimes troubles him, he still reads, paints and works on a daily basis, except when visitors from the art world or his friends and family demand his attention. Ever polite, and ever gracious, he has adapted his easy going ways to the nature and rhythms of those who make the pilgrimage to see the Dot Man.

George Andrews still refuses to travel outside of Georgia, although the offers grow in relationship to his expanding artistic reputation. He lives independently and maintains the routines that have sustained him, including reading his morning papers and visiting the Post Office, located on the Madison town square, each day. At the Post Office, his friends still call him "Gee" but others now address him as Mr. Andrews. To those in town who see only a slim older black man, wearing his cap and nodding politely, George Andrews has become a part of the fabric of Madison life.

George Andrews is a complex and determined individual whose spirit has sustained him through a difficult and challenging life. His son Benny, who certainly knows George well, has written about his father's personality, his public image and his artistic vision: "Often described by journalists as an 'impish fellow,' Dad, all of one hundred pounds or less, does have a cheery smile and a seemingly blessed, innocent aura about him. That's only one aspect of him though, believe me. Dad is a very complex container of much more than the casual observer sees or hears." As the "survivor of an almost unbelievable past" George has become "one of the most tenacious and imaginative persons" his son has known: "Ideas just bubble out of his head like lava… He's the personification of the mythical artist/poet who sees beauty through every pore, who is driven to create regardless of the circumstances."[34]

When asked by Benny about his recognition as an artist and if he would have preferred it at a younger age, George Andrews offered an interesting reply. "Well it would have been mighty nice when I was younger to get all this attention. I imagine I would have done a little travelling around, but now I'd just rather be at home here, painting or drawing something." When people ask how he is able to live alone, he replies: "'Well I got something to keep me company… All this artwork. It be on my mind. I lay down after saying my prayers, I get visions what to do." And, when asked if he gets lonesome, he responded: "When I ain't working on my art I do."[35]

So George Andrews, the Dot Man, still lives just off that highway to Plainview. His mother and his son rest in the Plainview Baptist Church graveyard. His children and his grandchildren have moved to Atlanta and beyond. The family cabin, where so many lives began, remains near the fields he once farmed. His father's plantation house, the old Orr Place, has been restored by its new owners to reflect the antebellum charm of Madison. He carries the history and spirit of these places with him, maintaining the family roots in Morgan County and awakens, each morning, with the rich possibilities of new visions and new paintings. The Dot Man's brush, it seems, is filled with paint and always ready. ●

N O T E S

A series of interviews with George Andrews and Benny Andrews, conducted from November of 1993 to June of 1994, and files of family materials and photographs owned by Benny Andrews served as primary sources for this essay and the accompanying exhibition.

1. *Benny Andrews, quoted in* Folk: The Art of Benny and George Andrews, *Memphis: Memphis Brooks Museum of Art, 1990, p. 28.*

2. *Raymond Andrews,* The Last Radio Baby, *Atlanta: Peachtree Publishers, Ltd., 1990, p. 64.*

3. *Eudora Welty, quoted in Charles Reagan Wilson, "Sense of Place,"* Encyclopedia of Southern Culture, *Chapel Hill: The University of North Carolina Press, 1989, p. 1137. See also William Ferris,* Local Color, A Sense of Place in Folk Art, *New York: McGraw-Hill, 1982.*

4. *Raymond Andrews,* The Last Radio Baby, *p. 24. This book serves as a valuable printed source for dates and information about the history of the Andrews family and the black history of Plainview and Madison, Georgia.*

5. *"George Andrews: Paintings and Objects," presented at The McIntosh Gallery, Atlanta, Georgia, May 5-July 1, 1994.*

6. *Alice Rae Yelen, "Self-Taught Artists: Who They Are," in* Passionate Visions of the American South, Self-Taught Artists from 1940 to the Present, *New Orleans: New Orleans Museum of Art, 1993, pp. 17-18.*

7. *Lucy Lippard,* Mixed Blessings, New Art in a Multicultural America, *New York: Pantheon Books, 1990, pp. 76-78.*

8. *Raymond Andrews,* The Last Radio Baby, *pp. 8-12. See also Raymond Andrews,* Rosiebelle Lee Wildcat Tennessee, *Atlanta: Peachtree Publishers, 1980.*

9. *Ibid., p. 16.*

10. *Benny Andrews, "George Andrews," in* Art Journal, *Spring 1994, Volume 53, Number 1, p. 22.*

11. *Ibid., p. 22.*

12. *Ibid., p. 22.*

13. *Ibid., p. 24.*

14. *Benny Andrews, unpublished written statement, February, 1985.*

15. *Viola Andrews, unpublished written statement, July, 1984.*

16. *Raymond Andrews,* The Last Radio Baby, *p. 78.*

17. *James Agee, quoted in Thomas W. Southall,* Of Time and Place, Walker Evans and William Christenberry, *San Francisco: The Friends of Photography, 1990, p. 8.*

18. *Raymond Andrews,* The Last Radio Baby, *foreword.*

19. *Benny Andrews, "Reminiscing with Ray,"* Habersham Review, *Spring 1994, Volume III, Number 1, p. 24.*

20. *Raymond Andrews,* The Last Radio Baby, *p. 180. Also confirmed in interviews with George Andrews, Benny Andrews and Viola Andrews in May and June of 1994.*

21. *Ibid., p. 180.*

22. *Ibid., p. 64.*

23. *Benny Andrews,* Habersham Review, *p. 26.*

24. *Raymond Andrews,* The Last Radio Baby, *p. 67.*

25. *Viola Andrews, Interview with the author, June 7, 1994.*

26. *George Andrews, unpublished written statement, December, 1984.*

27. *Patricia Bladon,* Folk, *p. 10.*

28. *George Andrews, unpublished written statement, 1984.*

29. *Ibid.*

30. *John Beardsley, "Spiritual Epics: The Voyage and the Vision in Black Folk Art," in* Black Folk Art in America, 1930-1980, *Washington: Corcoran Gallery of Art, 1982, p. 51.*

31. *Benny Andrews, unpublished written statement, February, 1985.*

32. *Raymond Andrews,* The Last Radio Baby, *p. 75.*

33. *Raymond Andrews, unpublished written statement, undated (c. 1985).*

34. *Benny Andrews, "George Andrews,"* Art Journal, *p. 24.*

35. *Ibid., p. 24.*

THE WORKS OF GEORGE ANDREWS

CALENDAR PAGE DOG

Oil painted frame and glass, 15½ x 22 in.

THE LAST SUPPER

Oil on cardboard collage image, 9 x 12 in.

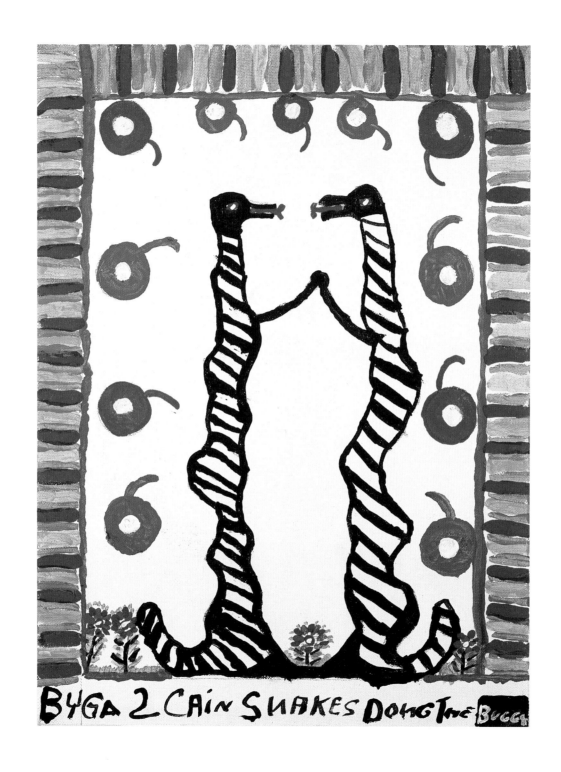

2 CAIN SNAKES DONG THE BUGGY

Oil on canvas board, 16 x 12 in.

THE PIG TREE

Oil on canvas board, 12 x 16 in.

SCRAMBLE ART

Oil on canvas board, 16 x 20 in.

I GOT ALL MY EYES ON YOU

Oil on canvas board, 16 x 20 in.

WOODEN CHAIR

Oil on wood, 38½ x 16½ x 18 in.

AFRICA QUEEN

Oil on canvas board, 14 x 11 in.

THE WHITE RABBIT MARRIED THE COLOR RABBIT

1989, Oil on canvas, 18 x 24 in.

THE VALLY OR DRY BONES

Oil on canvas board, 16 x 20 in.

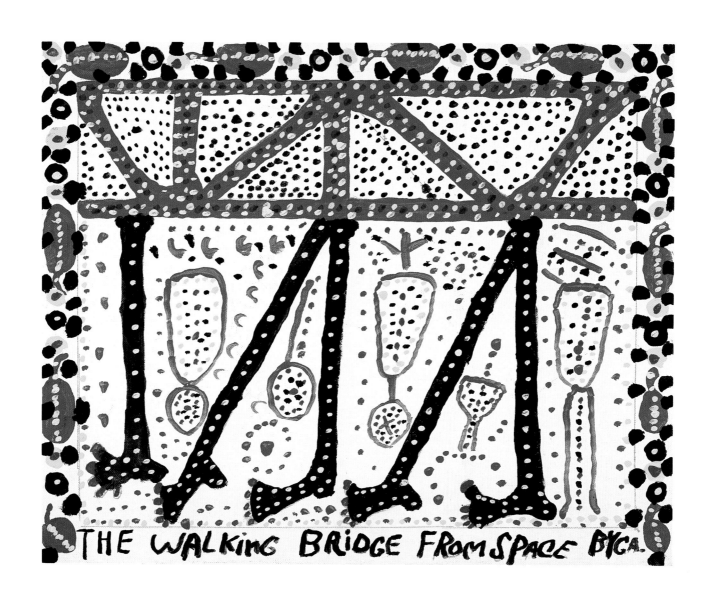

THE WALKING BRIDGE FROM SPACE

Oil on canvas board, 16 x 20 in.

THE ATLANTA CONSTITUTION
THE MORING PAPER
MY DAD LIKE HIS
PAPER HE WOOD
IN JOY READ IT BUT
HE PASSE BUT WAS
LOVE BY ALL WHO KNOW
HIM HIS NAME WAS
JAMES ORR BUT WAS
CALL MR JIM HE ONCE
WAS A BIG LAND
OWER WELL ALL
GOOD THING DO
COME TO AINN
SO BY BY
WE SEE YOU
BY GEORGE ANDREWS

MY DAD LIKE HIS PAPER (JAMES ORR)

1990, Oil on canvas, 42 x 32 in.

THIS IS BENNY ANDREWS

c. 1989, Oil on canvas, 36 x 22 in.

NENE HUMPHREY

1990, Oil on canvas, 36 x 24 in.

I LOVE YOU MOTHER DEAR (JESSIE ROSE LEE WILDCAT TENNESSEE)

1991, Oil on canvas, 46 x 25 in.

THIS IS THE ANDREWS FAMILY (ANDREWS FAMILY TREE)

1991, Oil on canvas, 60 x 40 in.

MY LOVIG WIFE (VIOLA ANDREWS)

1991, Oil on canvas, 42 x 25 in.

HARVEY ANDREWS

1991, Oil on canvas, 36 x 30¼ in.

SHIRLEY ANDREWS
1991, Oil on canvas, 36 x 20⅛ in.

VALERIA ANDREWS

1991, Oil on canvas, 32 x 22 in.

JOE (HAROLD ANDREWS)

1991, Oil on canvas, 36 x 20 in.

RAYMOND ANDREWS

1991, Oil on canvas, 35 x 24 in.

THE DOT MAN: GEORGE ANDREWS EXHIBITION CHECKLIST

PAINTINGS

1. THIS IS GEORGE ANDREWS
   O BOY HA HA
   1989, Oil on canvas, 50 x 44 in.

2. THIS IS THE ANDREWS FAMILY
   (ANDREWS FAMILY TREE)
   1991, Oil on canvas, 60 x 40 in.

3. VALERIA ANDREWS
   1991, Oil on canvas, 32 x 22 in.

4. JOE (HAROLD ANDREWS)
   1991, Oil on canvas, 36 x 20 in.

5. THIS IS BENNY ANDREWS
   c. 1989, Oil on canvas, 36 x 22 in.

6. RAYMOND ANDREWS
   1991, Oil on canvas, 35 x 24 in.

7. SHIRLEY ANDREWS
   1991, Oil on canvas, 36 x 20⅛ in.

8. NENE HUMPHREY
   1990, Oil on canvas, 36 x 24 in.

9. HARVEY ANDREWS
   1991, Oil on canvas, 36 x 30¼ in.

10. MY LOVIG WIFE
    (VIOLA ANDREWS)
    1991, Oil on canvas, 42 x 25 in.

11. I LOVE YOU MOTHER DEAR
    (JESSIE ROSE LEE WILDCAT
    TENNESSEE)
    1991, Oil on canvas, 46 x 25 in.

12. MY DAD LIKE HIS PAPER
    (JAMES ORR)
    1990, Oil on canvas, 42 x 32 in.

13. THE OLD ART ACE
    WITH HIS OLD BUDDY BRUSH
    Oil on canvas, 30 x 20 in.

14. THE LAST SUPPER
    Oil on cardboard collage image, 9 x 12 in.

15. CALENDAR PAGE DOG
    Oil painted frame and glass, 15½ x 22 in.

16. UNTITLED (WITCHDOCTOR)
    Oil and collage, 17 x 12 in.

17. MENS FROM SPACE
    WITH DEAD BIRD
    Oil on canvas, 15 x 19 in.

18. THE RUNNING VINE
    THAT RUN & RUN
    Oil on canvas, 15½ x 19½ in.

19. OUT IN SPACE
    IN A CRAY PLANTER
    Oil on canvas, 15 x 19 in.

20. MAN RUNS HIS MOUTH
    Oil on canvas board, 18 x 24 in.

21. PLEASE DONE BURN OLD GLORIA
    Oil on canvas board, 24 x 17 in.

22. THE WHITE RABBIT MARRIED
    THE COLOR RABBIT
    1989, Oil on canvas, 18 x 24 in.

23. THE POOR LITTLE GUN
    1989, Oil on canvas, 18 x 24 in.

24. HODOO STATUR
    Oil on canvas board, 8 x 10 in.

25. BULOONG DAY OF COLARS
    Oil on board, 20 x 16 in.

26. ALL YOU KIDS & TEEN AGES
    Oil on canvas board, 16 x 20 in.

27. THE TO LITTLE RATS
    LAST SUPPER
    Oil on canvas board, 16 x 20 in.

28. THE LITTLE GIRL
    Oil on canvas board, 20 x 16 in.

29. 2 KING SNAKES
    HAVE A LONE TALK
    Oil on canvas board, 11 x 14 in.

30. GRAND MAMA SINGS THE BLUES
    Oil on canvas board, 16 x 12 in.

31. THE WINE SAY TO THE MOON
    Oil on canvas board, 16 x 12 in.

32. BLACK IS BEAUTIFUL
    1986, Oil on canvas, 12 x 18 in.

33. THE SNAKE BAND BOYS
    1986, Oil on canvas, 12 x 18 in.

34. BOUTH MY APPLE EYES
    Oil on canvas, 12 x 18 in.

35. THE OLD PIGENS HOUSE
    Oil on canvas, 12 x 18 in.

36. THE OLD APPLE TREE
    Oil on canvas, 18 x 12 in.

37. JESUS ON THE CROOS
    1986, Oil on canvas, 18 x 12 in.

38. AT A SNAKE DANCE
    Oil on canvas, 14 x 16 in.

39. THE PIG TREE
    Oil on canvas board, 12 x 16 in.

40. A TORNADO BOUT
    TO TOUCH DOUWN
    Oil on board, 12 x 16 in.

41. THE KISSING PIGS
O BOY HAR HAR
Oil on canvas board, 12 x 16 in.

42. PLEAS DONE TRY
TO BUTTON ME DOWN
Oil on board, 12 x 16 in.

43. THE OLD INDIANS CAMP 1910
Oil on canvas board, 12 x 16 in.

44. AT THE IN ORE THE RAIN BOW
Oil on board, 11 x 14 in.

45. IN THE GOOD OLD DAYS
Oil on canvas board, 11 x 14 in.

46. UNTITLED (COLLAGE PHOTOS
WITH PAINTED LIPS AND EYES)
Oil on canvas board, 10 x 8 in.

47. UNTITLED (COLLAGE FACE
WITH PAINTED FEATURES)
Oil on canvas board, 10 x 8 in.

48. UNTITLED (RED HOUSE)
Oil and collage on board, 10 x 8 in.

49. COME ON AND TAKE A BITE
Oil on board, 12 x 9 in.

50. THIS IS THE LADDER
Oil on canvas board, 12 x 9 in.

51. CROSE OF PEACE
Oil on canvas board, 14 x 11 in.

52. AFRICA QUEEN
Oil on canvas board, 14 x 11 in.

53. THE VALLY OR DRY BONES
Oil on canvas board, 16 x 20 in.

54. 2 HOGS SKIS JUMPING O BOY
Oil on canvas board, 16 x 20 in.

55. I LOVE YOU OLD BLACK BOY
Oil on canvas board, 16 x 20 in.

56. I GOT ALL MY EYES ON YOU
Oil on canvas board, 16 x 20 in.

57. PEACE IN THE VALLY FOR ALL
Oil on canvas board, 16 x 20 in.

58. THE WALKING BRIDGE
FROM SPACE
Oil on canvas board, 16 x 20 in.

59. MY DEAR MOTHER FLOWERS BED
Oil on board, 16 x 20 in.

60. SCRAMBLE ART
Oil on canvas board, 16 x 20 in.

61. THE LONLY PAIRS SOCKS
Oil on board, 16 x 20 in.

62. I KNOW WHAT YOU ARE
YOU JEST A OLD SNAKE
Oil on canvas board, 16 x 20 in.

63. THE DEVIL AND HIS 2 SONS
Oil on board, 16 x 20 in.

64. 2 CAIN SNAKES
DONG THE BUGGY
Oil on canvas board, 16 x 12 in.

65. THE PIG SHOW AT THE FAIR
Oil on canvas board, 16 x 20 in.

66. THE DEVIL WIFE
Oil on board, 16 x 12 in.

67. THE 3 HEADS DEATH O BOY
Oil on canvas board, 9 x 12 in.

68. THE MOUNTN THAT GROWE
IN THE CLOUDY
Oil on board, 9 x 12 in.

OBJECTS

EIGHT PAINTED STYROFOAM TRAYS

- TWO SNAKES
  5¼ x 8⅛ in.

- FAN DESIGN
  8⅝ x 6¼ in.

- ANIMAL
  5¼ x 8¼ in.

- EYES IN WINE GLASS
  9½ x 7 in.

- LITTLE SISTER
  8 x 15 in.

- CROSS
  8 x 15 in.

- ROUND CIRCLES
  8 x 15 in.

- PIGS
  13⅞ x 9¾ in.

PAIR OF PAINTED BOOTS
  Oil on leather, 17 x 7 x 9 in.

FOUR PAIRS OF PAINTED SHOES

  A. GOLD
  Oil on vinyl, 5 x 7 x 9 in.

B. BLUE
Oil on vinyl, 3½ x 7 x 10 in.

C. BLUE
Oil on vinyl, 5 x 6½ x 10½ in.

D. BLACK
Oil on leather, 5½ x 7 x 8 in.

GREEN LANTERN
Oil on glass, 11 x 3 in.

BLUE LANTERN
Oil on glass, 17 x 6 x 7 in.

PAINTED PIG FIGURE
Oil on plaster, 19¼ x 14 x 18½ in.

PAINTED INDIAN FIGURE
Oil on plaster, 18 x 14 x 12 in.

PAINTED PURSE
*Oil on leather and canvas,
8½ x 11½ x 3½ in.*

PAINTED PURSE (SMALLER)
Oil on vinyl, 11 x 10 x 3 in.

SET OF PAINTED BLUE WARE:
TRAY AND TWO CONTAINERS

- SQUARE STOPPER JAR
Oil on glass, 4½ x 3 in.

- BLUE MASON JAR
Oil on glass, 4 x 3¼ in.

- BLUE PAINTED DISH
Oil on tin, 1¼ x 13 x 6½ in.

PAINTED ROCK WITH RED STRIPES
Oil on rock, 2½ x 4 x 3 in.

PAINTED TELEPHONE
Oil on plastic, 5 x 8 x 4 in.

PAINTED BASE
WITH EIGHT FLYING BIRDS
Oil on plaster, wire and plastic, 11 x 3½ in.

PAINTED HORSESHOE TRAY
Oil on ceramic, 1½ x 8½ x 7 in.

PAINTED PLATTER
"THE BLUE PLATE OF PEACE"
Oil on ceramic, 14 in. [diameter]

PAINTED CONTAINER WITH CHICKEN
Oil on stuffed fabric and metal, 22 x 9 in.

PAINTED DUCK
Oil on ceramic, 13 x 11 x 5 in.

PAINTED WALL CLOCK
Oil on wood, 23 x 10 x 5 in.

"IF YOUR UNDER 300 LB"
Oil on wooden chair, 32 x 19 x 18 in.

"PLEASE SIT DOWN OUT THE WAY"
Oil on wooden chair, 32 x 19 x 18 in.

WOODEN CHAIR
Oil on wood, 38½ x 16½ x 18 in.

"PLEASE SIT YOUR BOTTOM"
Oil on metal chair, 30 x 14 in.

"LOVE AND PEACE TO ALL"
Oil on metal table 20½ x 19 in. [diameter]

POT WITH PAINTED FLOWERS
*Oil on terra cotta and plastic
19 x 22 x 7 in.*

PAINTED VASE WITH FERN
Oil on glass, 19½ x 4 in.

PAINTED VASE WITH FLOWER
Oil on glass, 12 x 4½

PAINTED TRAY
AND TWO WHIRLIGIGS
*Oil on synthetic wood and plastic
20⅞ x 13¾ x 1¼ in. (tray)
19¼ x 8½ x 1 in. (whirligigs)*

PAINTED CARD TABLE
Oil on wood, 26 x 30 x 30 in.

PAINTED WHISKEY BOTTLES
Oil on glass, 11 x 3 in.

TWO MATCHING BRASS TRAYS
WITH PAINTED FRUIT
Oil on brass, 14¼ in. [diameter]

PAINTED ROUND PLATE
Oil on styrofoam, 9 in. [diameter]

PAINTED TURKEY PLATTER
Oil on ceramic, 11 x 18 in.

PAINTED JELLO MOLD
Oil on metal, 9¼ x 2 in.

PAINTED JELLO MOLD
Oil on metal, 8 x 3 in.

ASSORTED PAINTED BALLS

- LARGE RED FOOTBALL
Oil on rubber, 9½ x 5 x 5 in.

- SMALL RED FOOTBALL
Oil on rubber, 5½ x 3 x 3 in.

- ROUND RED BALL
Oil on rubber, 4 in. [circumference]

- SMALL BLACK FOOTBALL
Oil on plastic, 5½ x 3 x 3 in.

- SMALL BALL,
MULTI-COLORED ON BLACK
Oil on plastic, 3¼ in. [circumference]

- SMALL BALL, MULTI-COLORED ON WHITE
  Oil on plastic, 2¾ in. [circumference]

PAINTED BLUE COOLER TOP
Oil on plastic, 14 x 10 x 2 in.

FIGURE WITH CIGARETTE IN GOLD BOWL
Oil on plastic, fabric, 14½ x 5 x 5 in.

PAINTED BOWLS WITH DOLL INSIDE
Oil on glass and oil on plastic, plastic and fabric, 8 x 8¾ in.

PAINTED VASE AND BASE
Oil on milk glass (vase), 6¼ x 5 in.
Oil on metal (base), 8 x 4 in.

PAINTED BOWL WITH PAINTED SOFTBALL
Oil on ceramic and leather 5 x 8½ x 5 in.

PAINTED BOTTLE WITH CORK STOPPER
Oil on glass, 8¼ x 3½ in.

PAINTED PLASTIC CUP WITH RED RIBBON
Oil on plastic, paper, 3 x 3½ in. diameter

PAINTED TRIVET WITH ATTACHED BIRD
Oil on metal and ceramic,9¾ in. [diameter]

PAINTED CANDLE STAND WITH TINSEL
Oil metal, 3 x 6½ in.

PAINTED BOWL WITH PLASTIC FRUIT
Oil on plastic, 2¾ x 6¾ in.

PAINTED HAT
Oil on straw, 11 x 9 x 6 in.

PAINTED GOBLET
Oil on glass, 6¼ x 3½ in.

PAINTED BLACK BOWL WITH PAINTED BRASS MOLD
Oil on synthetic wood/plastic (bowl), 3 x 9¼ in.
Oil on metal (mold), 10½ x 5½ x 2¾ in.

PAINTED SHOE AND DOG PLANTER
Oil on ceramic, 4½ x 8 x 3¼ in.

PAINTED CEDAR SOUVENIR BOX
Oil on wood, 4¼ x 4 x 3 in.

PAINTED PLASTIC FRAME WITH OVERPAINTED IMAGE OF CHILD
Collage and oil on plastic, 7 x 6 x 1 in.

PAINTED HEXAGONAL CONTAINER WITH PAINTED BOWL
Oil on glass (container), 7½ x 5¼ [diameter]
Oil on tin (bowl), 2¼ x 5¼ in. [diameter]

SET OF FOUR PAINTED PLASTIC CUPS WITH STRAWS
Oil on plastic, 7 x 3 in.

YELLOW FLOWER AND BLUE FLOWER WHIRLIGIGS
Oil on plastic, 17½ x 12 x 2 in.

PAINTED LION PLANTER
Oil on ceramic, 7½ x 6½ x 7 in.

SMALL PAINTED BLACK AND WHITE DOG
Oil on ceramic, 3½ x 1½ x 5½ in.

MEDIUM PAINTED BLACK AND WHITE DOG
Oil on ceramic, 4½ x 2 x 7 in.

LARGE PAINTED BLACK AND WHITE DOG
Oil on ceramic, 6 x 4 x 9½ in.

PAINTED TRAY WITH FOUR FIGURES
Oil on brass, 9½ in. [diameter]

BLUE PAINTED ROUND TRAY
Oil on glass, 14 in. [diameter]

PAINTED BASKET WITH FLOWER
Oil on plastic, 5½ x 8 x 6½ in.

PAINTED BLACK TURTLE
Oil on rubber, 2½ x 4 x 6½ in.

PAINTED BLACK ALLIGATOR
Oil on rubber, 1¼ x 4¼ x 11½ in.

PAIR OF SMALL PAINTED WOODEN SHOES
Oil on wood, 2 x 4 x 4¼ in.

PAINTED DOLL SHOES
Oil on rubber, 4¼ x 4½ x 4½ in.

PAINTED CUP WITH RED BALL
Oil on metal and plastic, 4 x 3½ in.

PAINTED CUP WITH RED BALL
Oil on ceramic and plastic, 3½ x 3½ in.

PAINTED SHELL
Oil on shell, 2½ x 7 x 4 in.

All photography by Eric Olig except the following, used with permission from the collection of Benny Andrews: 4,6,9 (top), 20, 21, 22, 24 (all family photographs).

The Morris Museum of Art is a winner of the 1994-95 Regional Designation Award in the Humanities for "The Dot Man: George Andrews of Madison, Georgia." The awards were developed by the Atlanta Committee for the Olympic Games (ACOG) Cultural Olympiad to honor excellence and innovation in humanities programming throughout the South.